# I am BOLD Asian boy

⭐

## A Positive Affirmation Book for Asian Boys

WRITTEN BY
Yobe Qiu

ILLUSTRATED BY
Jade Le

Text copyright © 2023 Yobe Qiu
Illustrations copyright © 2023 Jade Le


All Rights Reserved. No part of this book may be reproduced in any form without the written permission of the copyright holders.

All inquiries including bulk purchase for promotional, educational, and business events, should be directed to hello@byyobeqiu.com

Published by By Yobe Qiu, Inc 2023

ISBN: 978-1-957711-10-2 (Paperback)
ISBN:978-1-957711-09-6 (Hardcover)


Book cover design and illustrations by Jade Le
www.jaesthetic.art

# Dedicated

Ba,

Thank you for your unconditional love and support, for being *selfless*, altruistic and the perfect role model for me.

Your Lucky Son,

Jason

I'm a **bold** Asian boy.

I'm confident and strong.
Whenever I feel shy,
I find a group where I belong.

SHOW & TELL

I'm a brave Asian boy.
I'm not afraid to try new things.

I wake ready for my day
Despite the changes it might bring.

I'm a **big-hearted** Asian boy.
I help out when I can,

even when the events aren't within my plan.

I'm a **brilliant Asian boy**.
I'm curious and love to learn.
I know it's okay to be wrong
I can always take multiple turns.

I'm a balanced Asian boy.
I'm excited for what my day brings.

From school to play to family,
I can juggle many things.

I'm a **blessed Asian boy.**
I am grateful for all I get.
I know that I am lucky,
and I will never forget.

I'm a beautiful Asian boy.
My eyes are perfect shapes.

I'm confident with my looks,
whether I wear shirts or capes.

I'm a bilingual Asian Boy.
I'm proud of who I am, and what I do.

My language, culture and traditions
and everything else, too!

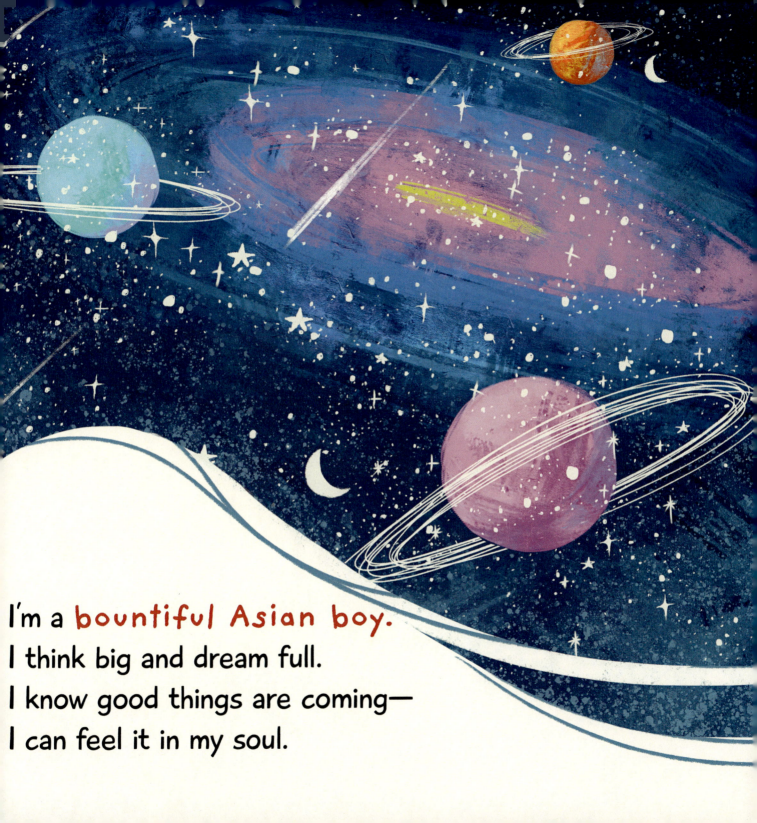

I'm a **bountiful Asian boy**.
I think big and dream full.
I know good things are coming—
I can feel it in my soul.

Yobe Qiu is an educator, entrepreneur, mom, and bestselling author with a passion for storytelling. As an educator, Yobe taught children and their families to embrace love and diverse cultures. When she identified a need for more multicultural books, she decided to create her own children's stories featuring Asian characters and cultures. Today, Yobe is proud to publish books that help children like her daughter feel seen, heard, and represented. Yobe looks forward to writing many more stories in the years to come.

*Author*

 hello@byyobeqiu.com    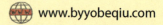 www.byyobeqiu.com

Jade is a full-time freelance illustrator living in the sunny island of Singapore with her husband and a nosey cat. She loves creating and drawing since she was little. Since 2019, she has assisted several talented authors to present their engaging stories in beautiful artworks. Jade hopes you will enjoy her artwork as much as she has fun illustrating it.

 jaesthetic.studio@gmail.com     www.jaesthetic.art

*Illustrator*

## OTHER TITLES BY YOBE QIU

» I am an Amazing Asian Girl

» I am a Magnificent Asian Mom

» Our Lunar New Year

» Our Moon Festival

*If you enjoyed this book, or any of Yobe Qiu's books, please leave a review. Your kindness and support are greatly appreciated!*

Made in the USA
Las Vegas, NV
28 April 2024